D1515304

Usborne
Animal Stories
for
Little Children

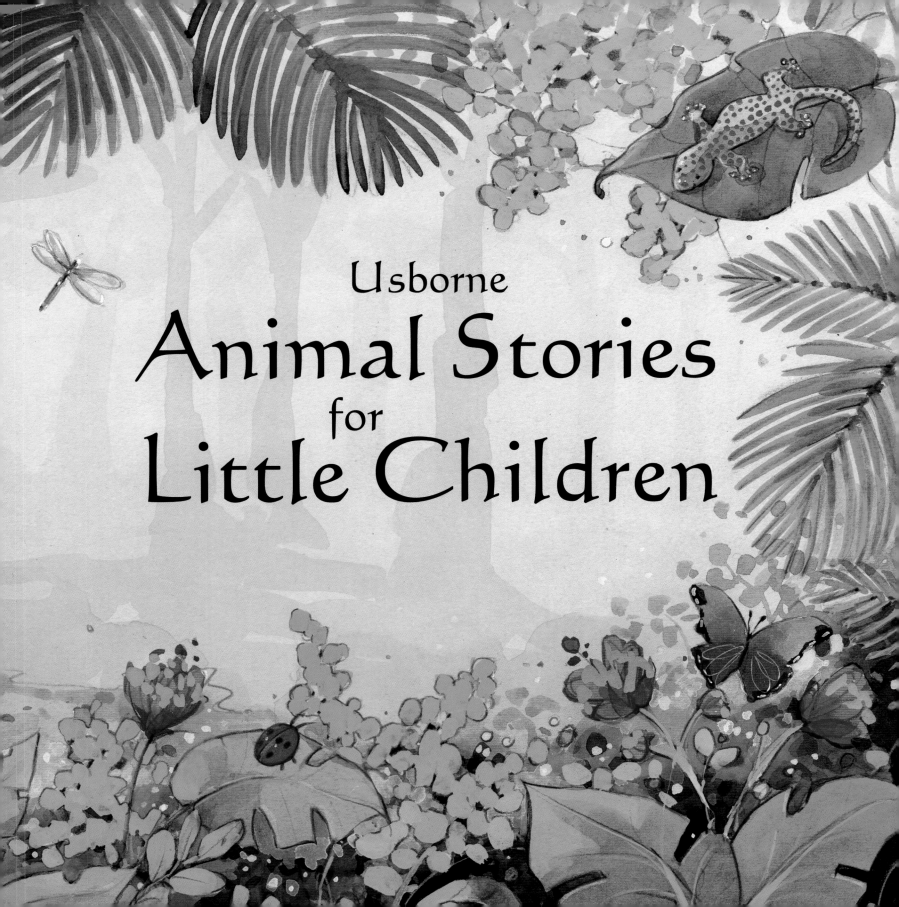

Animal Stories
Usborne
for
Little Children

Contents

How Elephants Lost their Wings

This is a story about

flying elephants,

two gods,

8

some houses,

proud peacocks

and banana trees.

9

You may not believe it but, once upon a time, elephants could fly.

And fly they did.
They flew all over the jungle.

11

They soared high
into the sky...

and zoomed
down to the
ground.

They even
looped
the loop.

Sometimes, the gods
sailed through the sky
on their backs.

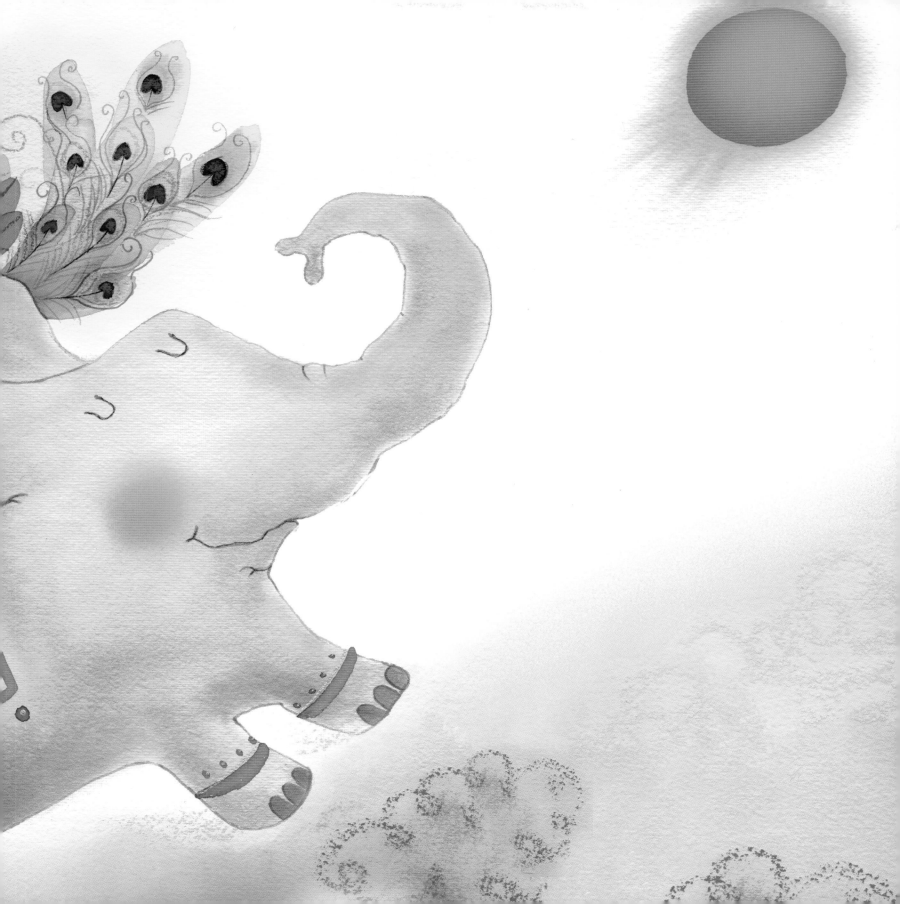

But the elephants were noisy.

They trumpeted, and
crowed like roosters.

16

Cock-a-
doodle-
doo!

Trees and houses
shook below them.

They collided with trees
and snapped them.

They crash-landed
on houses...

and flattened them.

Soon, all the trees were bent and broken...

and the houses were smashed to smithereens.

"We must stop them," said the gods, and they thought of a trick.

The gods invited the elephants
to a glorious, fruity feast.

The elephants slurped
and guzzled.

They
chomped...

...and they
gobbled.

When, at last, their tummies were full,
they slept.

While the elephants were snoring, the gods crept up and took away their wings.

They gave some to the peacocks,
to wear as splendid tails.

And they stuck some on
banana trees, giving them
huge green leaves.

25

When the elephants woke up,

they...

were...

FURIOUS!

They shouted and they stomped,
until the whole jungle quaked.

But their wings
were gone forever.

And they never flew again.

The Lion and the Mouse

One long, hot afternoon, Lion was snoozing in the shade.

32

When, pitter-patter, pitter-patter...
swish-swish...

...a little tail brushed
the tip of his nose.

Aaaaaa-chooooooooooooo!!! sneezed Lion.

He awoke with a start.

35

"How dare you disturb me!" Lion snarled at a terrified mouse.

"I'm so sorry," stammered the mouse.
"I didn't mean to... I didn't realize..."

"Do you know what I do to those who wake me?" Lion roared.

"I eat them up!"

"Please don't eat me," begged the mouse.

"Spare my life today and maybe, one day, I'll save yours."

"YOU?" scoffed Lion. "What could you ever do to help me?"
"Run along, little mouse. I'm laughing too much to eat you."

And the mouse ran - as fast as she could.

The very next day, Lion walked straight into a hunter's trap.

He roared and he struggled, but the more he struggled, the tighter the trap became.

"I'm stuck," he realized. "I'll never get out!"

But the little mouse heard his cries.

45

She rushed to his side.
"Don't worry," she squeaked.
"I've come to save you."

"What can you do?" groaned Lion.
"You're much too small to help me."

The mouse ignored him, and set to work.
She nibbled and gnawed at the gnarly old ropes.

She nibbled all day and all night.

At last, as the sun rose in the sky, Lion was free once more.

"You saved me!" said Lion, holding her gently in his paw. "I was wrong to laugh at you, little mouse."

"I see little friends can be great friends, after all."

Brer Rabbit
and the
Blackberry Bush

Once upon a time, Brer Rabbit was lazing around, dreaming up ways to trick...

Brer Fox...

who was busy planning
tricks of his own.

You see, Brer Rabbit and
Brer Fox were sworn enemies.

Take this!
You fiendish fox!

Take that! You
rascally rabbit!

Brer Fox's latest trick was to set a clever trap.

The next morning, Brer Rabbit was happily lolloping along, lippety-loppitty, lippety-loppitty, when...

59

TWANG!

He was
snapped up
in the trap.

If I can just...

Uh-oh!

61

"Ha, ha! Got you!"
mocked Brer Fox.

He licked
his chops.

"Now I'm going
to gobble you up!"

Brer Rabbit thought fast.
"Yipee!" he cried, sounding
full of glee.

"You WANT me to eat you?"
asked Brer Fox.

"Oh yes! I'm so delicious,"
sang Brer Rabbit.

"Fry me...

boil me...

...bake me in
a pie!"

"But please, please,
PLEASE...

whatever you do, don't throw me in the
scary, spiky, b-b-b-blackberry bush!"

"Now, that's an idea... "
grinned Brer Fox.

He grabbed
Brer Rabbit
by the ears.

He hurled him
through the air.

Brer Rabbit
whizzed around
like a whirligig...

And landed...

SPLAT! in the middle of the blackberry bush.

Whew!

"Hee, hee, hee!"
cried Brer Rabbit.

"I was born in the blackberry bush. It can't hurt me."

"I know my way around it like the back of my paw."

Brer Fox ground
his teeth
in rage.

While lippity-loppitty, lippity-loppitty, Brer Rabbit skipped his way home.

The Little Red Hen

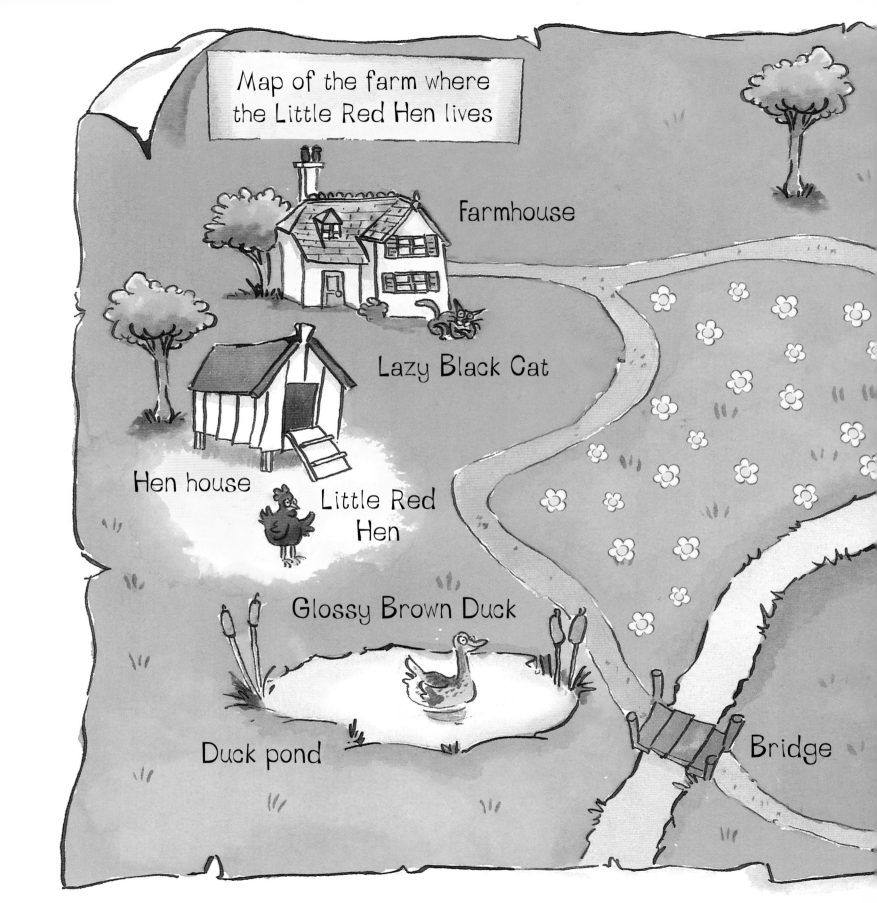

Map of the farm where the Little Red Hen lives

Farmhouse

Lazy Black Cat

Hen house

Little Red Hen

Glossy Brown Duck

Duck pond

Bridge

Barn

Great Fat Rat

N
W   E
S

Field

Stream

Mill

Bakehouse

Once upon a time, there was a little red hen.

Cheep! Cheep!

Pecketty-peck!

She lived on a farm in a
little white hen house with
a bright red roof.

The little red hen
had three best
friends.

Meeeow!

A lazy black cat
who lived in the farmhouse.

Quack!

A glossy brown duck
who lived on the pond.

And a great fat
rat who lived in
the barn.

Squeak!

One morning, the little red hen walked to the field.

She was looking for juicy worms to eat.
She scratched around with her busy little feet...

Hide! It's the little red hen.

and found some
grains of wheat.

"Ooh!" she cried. She fluffed her feathers.

"Who will help me plant the wheat?"

"Not I," said the cat.

87

"Not I," said
the duck.

"Not I," said
the rat.

"Fine!" said the
little red hen.
"Then I'll do it myself."

And she did.

88

The little red hen pecked at
the ground and made a hole.

What a waste of time.

One by one,
she dropped in
the grains.

The little red hen waited
for her wheat to grow all
through the winter.

First, the shoots were small and green.

By spring, the shoots were tall and strong.

91

In summer, they turned from green to gold.

At last, the wheat was ready.

"Who will help
me cut it down?"
said the little red hen.

"Not I,"
said the cat.

"Not I,"
said the duck.

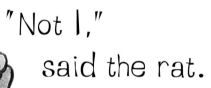

"Not I,"
said the rat.

"Fine!" said the little red hen.
"Then I'll do it myself."

And she did.

She cut down the wheat without
any help at all.

"Who will help me take
the wheat to the mill?"
said the little red hen.

"Not I," said
the cat.

"Not I,"
said the duck.

"Not I," said the rat.

"Fine!" said the little red hen. "Then I'll take it to the mill myself!"

And she did.

She took the wheat to the mill
and ground it into flour,
without any help
at all.

"Who will help me make the flour into bread?"
said the little red hen.

"Not I," said
the cat.

"Not I," said the duck.

"Not I," said
the rat.

"Then I'll make it myself,"
said the little red hen.

And she did.

She baked the bread without any help at all.

"Who will help me eat the bread?" said the little red hen.

The cat, the duck and
the rat jumped up.

"Mmm," they said, as they smelled the bread.

The bread was warm and soft.

"I'll have a slice," said the duck.

"I'll take two," said the cat.

"Oh no you won't!" said the little red hen.

"I'll eat it ALL BY MYSELF!"

And she did.

The Little Giraffe

Once, there was a little giraffe.

He was the very first
giraffe in the world.

He lived on the great plains
of East Africa...

...with his best friend, Rhino.

Every day, they searched for food.

But the sun was hot. The earth was dry.

The ground cracked.
Plants withered and died.

"I know!" said the little giraffe, at last. "Let's see the wise man. He'll know what to do."

We're hungry.

Please can you help?

"Come back tomorrow," said the wise man.

"I'll make you a
magic drink."

123

The next day, the little giraffe
trotted back to the wise
man's house.

"Hello!" said the wise man.
"Your magic drink is ready.
But where's Rhino?"

"I don't know," said the little giraffe.
"I couldn't find him anywhere."

"Then it's all for you," said the wise man and he put down a bowl.

The drink bubbled and fizzed. The little giraffe lapped it up.

He felt a shiver in his spine and a tingling in his hooves.

Slowly, his legs began to grow...

Then his neck
s-t-r-e-t-c-h-e-d out.

"I'm tall!" he cried.

"Now you can reach the leaves high in the trees,"
said the wise man.

But where was Rhino?
He was busy munching some dry grass that he had found.

Mmmm...

He had forgotten all about the wise man.

"There you are,"
said the not-so-little giraffe.

What happened
to you?

"I drank the magic drink," he told Rhino.
"Can I have some?" Rhino asked eagerly.

The little giraffe shook his head sadly.
"I'm sorry," he said. "There's none left."

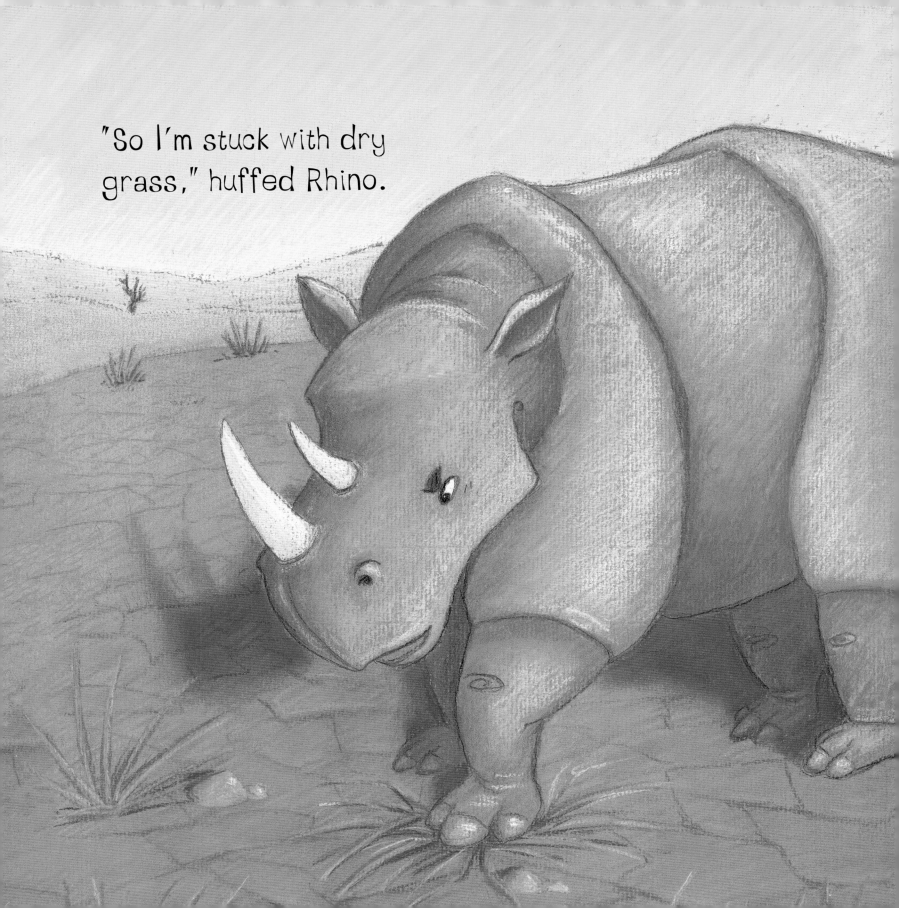

"So I'm stuck with dry grass," huffed Rhino.

"And you get to eat juicy green leaves," he growled, glaring at the oh-so-tall giraffe.

"It's not fair!" he thought, angrily.

132

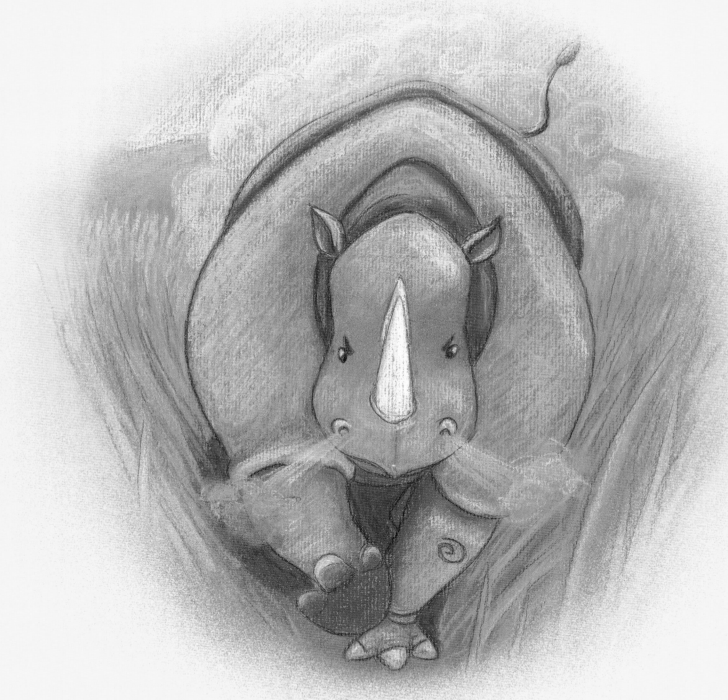

And that is why you should never get too close to a rhino.
They are still angry today!

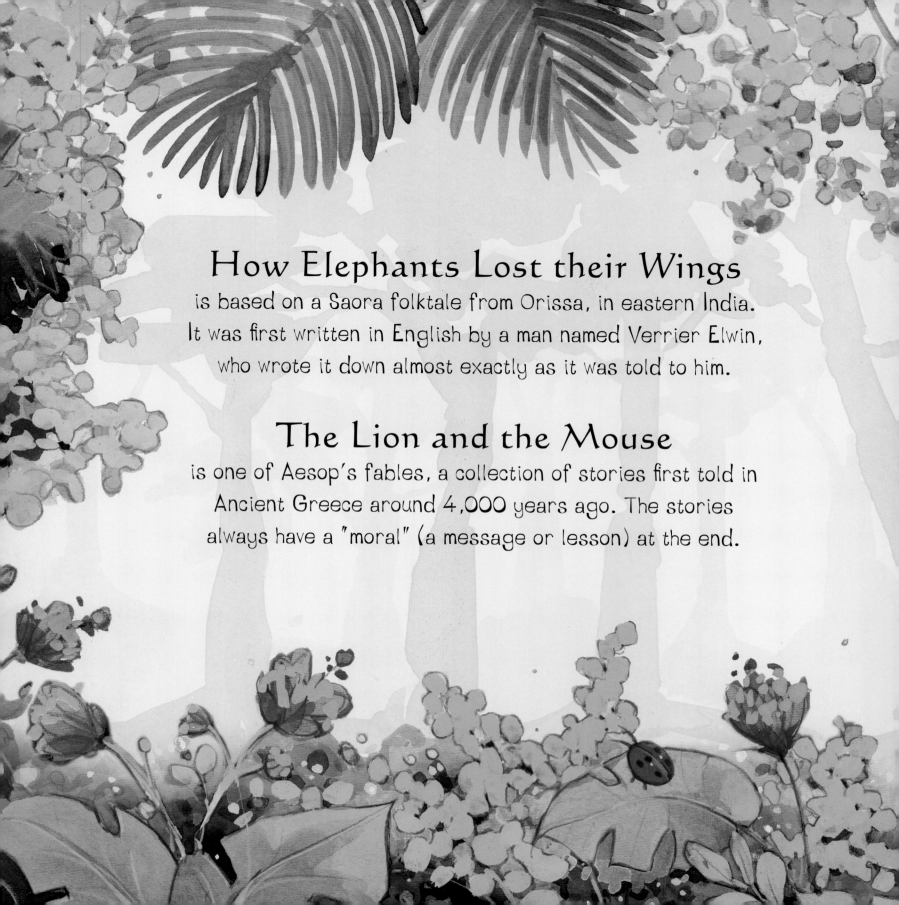

How Elephants Lost their Wings

is based on a Saora folktale from Orissa, in eastern India.
It was first written in English by a man named Verrier Elwin,
who wrote it down almost exactly as it was told to him.

The Lion and the Mouse

is one of Aesop's fables, a collection of stories first told in
Ancient Greece around 4,000 years ago. The stories
always have a "moral" (a message or lesson) at the end.

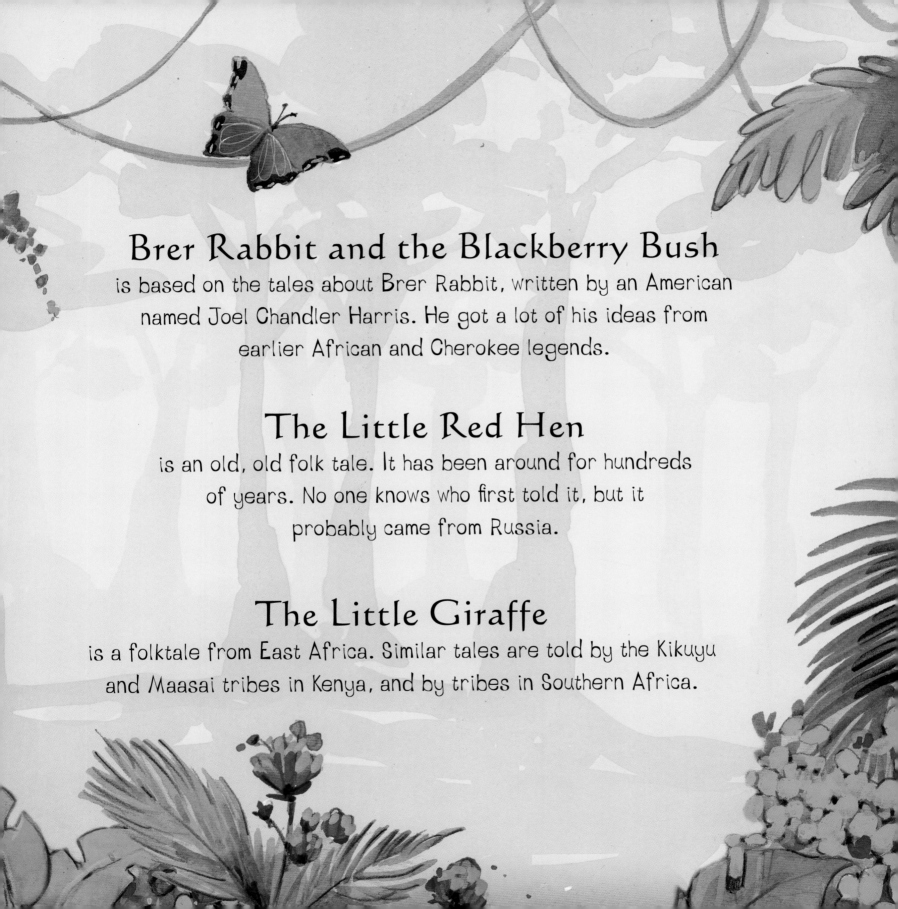

Brer Rabbit and the Blackberry Bush

is based on the tales about Brer Rabbit, written by an American named Joel Chandler Harris. He got a lot of his ideas from earlier African and Cherokee legends.

The Little Red Hen

is an old, old folk tale. It has been around for hundreds of years. No one knows who first told it, but it probably came from Russia.

The Little Giraffe

is a folktale from East Africa. Similar tales are told by the Kikuyu and Maasai tribes in Kenya, and by tribes in Southern Africa.

Edited by Jenny Tyler,
Lesley Sims and Susanna Davidson
Designed by Caroline Spatz, Louise Flutter,
Michelle Lawrence and Samantha Meredith
Cover design by Russell Punter
Additional illustration by Victoria Ball
Digital manipulation by John Russell

First published in 2009 by Usborne Publishing Ltd, 83-85 Saffron Hill, London EC1N 8RT,
England. www.usborne.com Copyright © 2009 Usborne Publishing Ltd.
The name Usborne and the devices 🏆⚛ are Trade Marks of Usborne Publishing Ltd.
All rights reserved. No part of this publication may be reproduced, stored in a retrieval
system, or transmitted in any form or by any means, electronic, mechanical,
photocopying, recording or otherwise, without the prior permission of the publisher.
First published in America in 2009. UE. Printed in Shenzhen, Guangdong, China.